SU

OREP
EDITIONS

15, rue de Largerie - 14480 CULLY
Tél: 02 31 08 31 08 - Fax: 02 31 08 31 09
E-mail: info@orep-pub.com - **Web: www.orep-pub.com**

Editor: Philippe Pique
Layout: Sophie Youf
English translation : Heather Costil

Graphic design: OREP
ISBN : 978-2-915762-62-4 - Copyright OREP 2008
All rights reserved – Legal deposit: 1st quarter 2008
Printed in France

Photo credits: IWM – London. ECPA – Paris. Karl Althoff- Zweibrücken. Bundesarchiv – Militärarchiv . Cabinet des Estampes – BN – Paris. National Archives – Washington. The National Archives – Ottawa. Dite – USIS – Paris. Smithonian Institution – Washington.

Bibliography: Diren – Les jardins de la mémoire. Les hommes et leur destin – Ed. Orep – 1999. Joseph Balkoski, Omaha beach: D-Day, June 6, 1944 – Ed. Stackpole Books, Mechanicsburg, Pennsylvania, 2004. Charles Taylor, Omaha Beachhead, Washington DC, OCMH, 1984. Gordon Harrison, Cross-Channel attack, Washington DC, OCMH, 1951.

INTRODUCTION

OMAHA, POINTE DU HOC AND THE AMERICAN CEMETERY

In November 1943, the American landing on Tarawa Island, defended by the Japanese, and during which 5,000 Marines were put out of action, had been a great shock to the American people and had even caused heated controversy throughout the country. What would become of them when facing the Germans on the Channel coast, where the allied chiefs had planned to launch a vast amphibious operation in the spring of 1944? Similarly to Tarawa Atoll, where the Marines, totally exposed, had to cross the gap between the coral reefs and the beach, the Normandy coast would also force the American troops to penetrate, uncovered, a vast beach riddled with mines and traps, and swept with enemy gunfire from secure and invisible bunkers. Horrendous carnage was surely to be expected.

Those of us who know the story of the assault on Omaha Beach on the 6th of June 1944, are well aware of the bloody battle that took place there; however, as soon as the initial crisis was under control, the survivors proved to be unshakeable and, as early as the very evening of D-Day, they forced the German defence to retreat from the coastal fortifications that formed the Atlantic Wall.

Together with Guadalcanal and Iwo Jima in February 1945 and the island of Okinawa, two months later, the successful landing on Omaha Beach against the German Wehrmacht troops, is one of modern American history's most glorious events. The capture of the German coastal artillery battery at Pointe du Hoc, in the early hours of the 6th of June, is another of Operation Overlord's exceptional achievements, and is a fine example of audacity and courage.

The vast memorial in Colleville-sur-Mer, where some 10,000 American soldiers are laid to rest, is a constant reminder of their ultimate sacrifice at Omaha, the first step towards the second front and the liberation of Europe.

■ High view: Landing on Omaha Beach
■ Low view: Omaha Beach and the American Cemetery

It was as early as January 1943, at the Casablanca Conference, that Roosevelt and Churchill decided to challenge the Reich on the European continent by means of a vast landing operation. In order to establish the outline plan for the future invasion on the north-western European coastline, in the spring of 1944, both allied heads of state created a special staff to be known as « Cossac ». Comprising a thousand British and American strategists from three military services, this brain trust commanded by General Morgan was to devise the plans for one of the greatest operations the 20th Century had ever seen and whose aim was to change the course of history by putting an end to the Reich's domination and by restoring democracy throughout the continent.

THE AMERICAN PLAN OF ATTACK

Six months later, General Morgan presented the civil and military authorities with his project for the allied army return into Western Europe. His plan involved a massive amphibious attack, in early May 1944, on the Normandy coastline facing the English Channel, in the heart of the Seine Bay and far from any continental port, thanks to the construction of an artificial harbour. Two of the three Calvados beaches originally planned by Morgan,

■ Landing off Saint-Laurent on D-Day

■ Point du Hoc battery observation post

stretching from Courseulles-sur-Mer to Isigny-sur-Mer, were to be attacked by the British and the third (later to be known as Omaha), initially codenamed « Beach 313 », by the Americans. Later, in early 1944, following orders from Eisenhower and Montgomery, the assault zone was to be enlarged encompassing two further beaches: Sword (in the vicinity of Ouistreham) and Utah (at the foot of the Cotentin peninsula). Requiring added preparation, the extension of the bridgehead was to delay the allied attack by one month.

The US V Corps

General Marshall chose the 1st US Army commanded by General Bradley to conduct the assault on the two beaches assigned to the Americans, then to take control of the port of Cherbourg and the major road junction at Saint-Lô. This military formation comprised two major units: the V Corps (General Gerow) in charge of the assault on Omaha and the capture of Saint-Lô, together with the VII Corps (General Collins) in charge of operations on Utah Beach and the control of the port of Cherbourg.

■ The American Cemetery with warships in the background (6th June 1944)

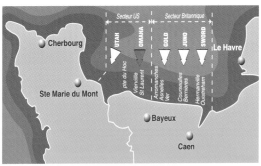

■ The five landing beaches

General Gerow

A t the age of 56, General Gerow, boasting two stars on his helmet, had commanded the 29th Infantry Division up to his nomination as chief of the V US Army Corps in July 1943. Gerow was a very strict yet loyal and competent man and his friends, Eisenhower and Bradley, were the only two people allowed to address him without calling him General. To compensate for his lack of combat experience, he studied in detail previous amphibious attacks carried out by the Allied forces in Africa, Sicily, Italy and in the Pacific, paying particular attention to the operation that had caused great losses among the Marines on Tarawa beach.

Gerow was far from being a pessimist, but he was realistic. He knew that during landings, defending troops were always at an advantage over their assailants arriving via the sea and that such operations involved great risks. Had they not come close to disaster at Salerno and Anzio in Italy? How were operations likely to unfold on the Channel coast, where the Germans had been given sufficient time to prepare for the attack? Sheltered in bunkers and trenches, the enemy was all-powerful and in order to force it to retreat Gerow needed to plan a frontal attack on the defensive positions that had been set up in the gullies and the ravines separating the beach from the inland territories. Such an offensive attack against the Atlantic Wall fortifications, similar to those launched at Verdun in 1916, would surely be

■ From left to right: Bradley, Gerow, Eisenhower, Collins

costly and success was far from guaranteed. To accomplish their mission on the 6th of June 1944, the V Corps comprised two infantry divisions, the 1st and the 29th, reinforced by two Rangers regiments, totalling around 35,000 men.

The 1st Division, the « Big Red One »

F ormed in 1917, the 1st Division already boasted two successful landing operations: Torch in North Africa in November 1942 and Husky in Sicily in July 1943. Repatriated to Great Britain in August 1943 to prepare for Operation Overlord, the unit was placed under the command of General Clarence Huebner, a World War I veteran. Nicknamed the « Big Red One », the 1st Division's recruits were from the « melting-pot » in the vicinity of New York, their names were of European origin (Italian,

116TH INFANTRY REGIMENT

■ *First infantry regiment to land on the Vierville sector*

German, Czech, Polish...) and they arrived in successive swarms at the American Army training base situated on the English coast. Like all infantry units, the division comprised 14,300 troops divided into three regiments, each of them with 3,100 men. These regiments (16th, 18th and 28th) were in turn comprised of three battalions each with 870 men, each battalion being divided into four companies, each with 215 GI's. Specialised support troops were also assigned to the 1st Division for the Channel attack (engineers, artillery, reconnaissance, transmissions, police and medical staff). On the morning of D-Day, the 16th Infantry Regiment, commanded by Colonel George Taylor, was, alongside the 116th Infantry Regiment and the 29th Division, the first unit to set foot on Omaha Beach. The 1st division was Bradley's favourite unit; having already taken part in amphibious assaults and with combat experience, the division's staff had proven capable of keeping a cool head in chaotic battles and crisis situations.

◀ ■ Colleville-sur-Mer. Monument in memory of the 1st US Infantry Division

■ Vierville-sur-Mer ▶ Monument in memory of the 29th US Infantry Division

The 29th Division « Twenty-Nine let's go »

Contrary to the 1st Division, the 29th had no experience of combat. The division comprised rookies, enlisted in 1941 and originating from the states of Maryland, Virginia and Pennsylvania, together with officers from American military academies including West Point. In September 1942, the Twenty-Nine commanded by General Gerow, took up quarters in Great Britain. It was the 4th American Division to cross the Atlantic. Following Gerow's promotion to commander of the V Corps, the division was placed under the orders of General Charles Gerhard.

In order to improve its fighting potential and to try to approach the standard of the 1st Division, the 29th was subjected to severe military training (marches, manoeuvres, embarkation and landing exercises, demolition techniques, mine clearance and use of special weapons such as flamethrowers). Hence, the basic infantryman who, hitherto, only knew how to shoot a rifle or a machine gun, was transformed into an infantry sapper, an assault specialist and a « super fighter ». On the morning of the 6th of June, facing Vierville-sur-Mer, the 116th Infantry Regiment of the 29th Division, was, despite major losses, to demonstrate both initiative and determination, just as General Gerow had asked them to in his message, « Hit hard and keep going forward... we fight on God's side and cannot fail. Good luck »

Preparations and preliminary bombings

Flat, sandy and approximately 7 kilometres long, Omaha beach forms a harmonious curve stretching from Colleville to Vierville. Along this part of the coast, domi-

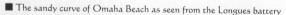

■ The sandy curve of Omaha Beach as seen from the Longues battery

■ View of Omaha beach and the slope overlooking the sea in June 1944

nated by cliffs, it is the only suitable shore for a major amphibious operation. Access from the beach to the inland plateau is via a 40 metre high escarpment. From the beach, the only routes providing access to the villages of Vierville, Saint-Laurent and Colleville, situated less than a kilometre away, are those following the gullies cutting into the vast embankment that overlooks the high seas.

The initial attack on Omaha was to be carried out by two infantry regiments (the 16th and the 116th) which were to land in successive waves. Once they had set foot on the sand, the aim of these troops was to diminish German defence using the guns and amphibious tanks landed a few minutes earlier, to create and mark navigation corridors among the obstacles on the beach to enable barges to deliver reinforcements and supplies to the top of the beach at high tide, to penetrate inland via

gullies towards the main Caen - Cherbourg road (the RN13) whilst dispersing to join the British troops landed on Gold Beach to the left, and the 4th Division on Utah Beach to the right.

For the purposes of the attack, the command had divided Omaha Beach into four sectors nicknamed Charlie-Dog-Easy-Fox, which were in turn divided into subsectors each of a different colour.

Different units had been assigned each of the eight subsectors with a specific objective and following a strictly timed programme. The Rangers had been assigned the capture of the radar station at Point de la Percée, together with the neutralisation of the coastal artillery battery at Pointe du Hoc, two German strong points situated a few kilometres to the west of Omaha.

During the first hour of the attack on Omaha, General Gerow had planned to land a total of just over 4,000 men, in other words, according to the allied information service, six to seven times the German defence troops.

Before the assailants arrived on the beach, allied planes would already have bombed the German coastal defence several times throughout the night and, by the early hours of the morning, the US Navy would have taken over from its massive warships anchored in the high seas. The « Top brass » from the V Corps staff reckoned that under such an avalanche of attack, the enemy defences would be shaken, the mine fields destroyed and their adversary demoralised. And that wasn't all! Just before the arrival of the first group, a fleet of landing barges, some of them equipped with rocket launcher tubes, others with guns, were to carry out close bombing on the beach and to overwhelm the coastal defences during the approach of the landing craft (LCA, LCM and LCT) bringing the first assault troops and their equipment.

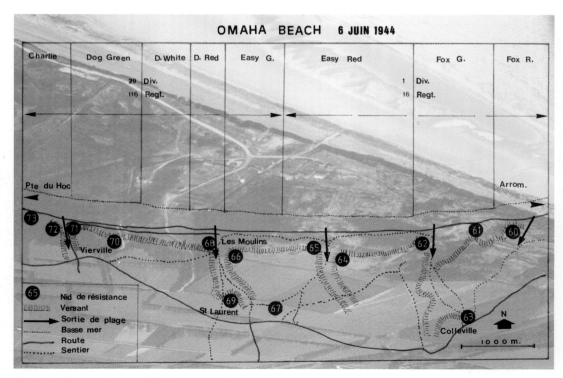

■ Omaha: German defences and US plan of attack Background photo: Gully cutting into the Colleville-sur-Mer beach escarpment

THE GERMAN DEFENCE STRATEGY

As we already know, from Arromanches to the mouth of the River Vire, stretching over around 30 kilometres as the crow flies, the coast is formed of alternating cliffs and low beaches. Whereas a landing operation at the foot of the high chalky cliffs of the Bessin or in the marshlands of the Vire estuary was impracticable, the vast beach stretching from Colleville to Vierville, offered, on the contrary, a particularly propitious environment. And that is precisely why the occupying German forces had taken great care to defend these shores.

Festung Europa (the European fortress)

LThe German command had ensured the defence, not only of the escarpment, but also of the beach foreshore. As a matter of fact, the most imposing defence structures were concentrated on the summit of the plateau dominating the high seas, just above the access to the gullies that cut into the huge embankment. Mortars, grenade launchers and old tank turrets were scattered around the small concrete forts (referred to as bunkers by the Germans and pillboxes by the Americans), equipped with antitank guns that scoured the beach. Connected to one another via a network of trenches, these strong points collectively comprised what the Germans referred to as a Widerstandsnest (resistance nest) abbreviated to WN. There were around fifteen WNs from Vierville to Colleville, located in such a manner that they prevented any assailant from entering into the gullies providing the only access inland. Gaining control of these beach exits was the very basis of General Gerow's plan of attack. Without these gateways, no vehicle could leave the beach and no landing operation could ever succeed if, following the initial assault, the caravans of caterpillar-tracked vehicles, trucks and jeeps could not make their way inland as quickly as possible.

In between the gullies, defence of the embankment was, to a large extent, neglected, suggesting that the Germans did not believe it was possible to scale the precipice. Nonetheless, after the failure of murderous attempts to penetrate the German defence at the gully entrance, the American troops eventually gave up the initial battle plan, deciding to climb the steep ridge and to attack the fortifications from the rear.

■ Obstacles on Omaha Beach

Thousands of obstacles on the shore

Since Hitler's nomination, late 1943, from Rommel as inspector of coastal fortifications, then head of anti-invasion operations, the shoreline had become the Hauptkampflinie (Rommel's main line of resistance). It was at a time when he had not yet gathered all of his combat resources, when he was in a vulnerable position, that the enemy had to be thrown back to the sea. Hence, as from early 1944, Omaha Beach, just like all of the other beaches bordering the Channel, was progressively covered with a forest of obstacles of all sorts (stakes, tetrahedrons, lengths of railway track...) most often dressed with a mine and metallic teeth aimed at tearing open the hulls of landing craft. However, despite the fact that defence operations had not yet been completed in June 1944, existing resources were sufficient to oblige the allied command to organise their lan-

ding at low tide, hence exposing their troops, during the beach crossing, to automatic gunfire from the defending occupiers. Such a direct attack was sure to cost many lives; Gerow could therefore expect heavy losses.

■ Antitank obstacle positioned on Omaha Beach

OMAHA BEACH

The 716th Division

The 716th Division was one of the 60 German divisions stationed on the Western front. The division, in fact, belonged to the 7th Army, a major military formation occupying both Brittany and Normandy. Further afield, to the north of the Seine, was the 15th Army. Commanded by General Richter whose command post was located in Caen, the 716th Division's mission since 1942 had been to defend the Calvados coastline from the River Orne to the River Vire, across a distance of around 80 kilometres. Similarly to the majority of divisions in charge of the Festung Europa (European fortress) coastal defence, the 716th was a static unit with no modern

■ General Richter, commander of the 716th Infantry Division

means of transport at its disposal. Equipped with horse-drawn carts, this division comprised around 8,000 men, most of them either very young recruits or relatively old soldiers, or even a number of crippled veterans from the Russian front. To complete its manpower, the division's command had sent two Georgian battalions said to be volunteers. The division's weaponry was ill-assorted and partly composed of plundered guns, which proved problematic when it came to finding spare parts.

According to the Intelligence (the allied command's information service), only one of the 716th Division's battalions, comprising 600 men, was in charge of arming the fifteen fortified strong points scattered across the 7 kilometres separating Colleville and Vierville. The service's secret report added that, given the length of the front defended by the division and the dispersal of its troops, the arrival of massive reinforcements was highly unlikely. We will discover later that this estimation of the enemy forces was quite inaccurate.

■ Rommel inspecting the Osttruppen (Eastern European volunteers)

6 JUNE 1944, THE ASSAULT ON OMAHA

The first influx of allied troops was to set foot on French soil at 6.30am, with the first light of day and the rising tide and immediately following bombardments by the 8th Air Force and the US Navy aimed at neutralising the Atlantic Wall defences. The failed aerial and naval bombings, one of the reasons for the great difficulty encountered by the infantrymen on the beach, will be discussed later.

As planned, the first wave of attack (1,500 men), transported by fifty landing craft, landed on time on the 7 kilometre stretch of Omaha Beach: the 16th Infantry Division (1st Division), on the eastern portion (sub-sectors Easy and Fox) and the 116th Infantry Division (29th Division) on the western portion. Over and above these two regiments, a Ranger battalion, whose mission was to capture the radar station located at Pointe de la Percée, was landed on the narrow beach codenamed Charlie and situated to the extreme west of Omaha.

Barely had the men from the 29th Division set foot on the shore, when hellfire from the resistance nests, apparently intact despite previous bombings, decimated the infantrymen from the 116th Regiment's A Company in charge of clearing the beach exit at Vierville. The road in question, tarred and of good quality, was the most interesting exit Omaha Beach had to offer. Simultaneously, the troops that had planned to land facing Hamel au Prêtre, immediately to the left of Vierville, had drifted eastwards in the strong current, finally to land in front of the Moulins valley. Just as in Vierville, the defenders waited until everyone was on the beach before pulling their triggers, hence launching their terrible carnage. Bushes on the imposing embankment had been set on fire by Navy shells and the resulting cloud of smoke enabled surviving assailants to run to shelter at the foot of a long shingled ridge. Any attempt to approach the valley of Les Moulins, in an effort to provide another exit point, would be pure suicide under such intense enemy fire from fortified and well-camouflaged bunkers.

■ Omaha Beach: Dog Red and Easy Green sectors (Moulin valley entrance)

The soldiers therefore stayed put, hiding, paralysed by the mine-ridden terrain.

At the same time, 750 men from the 16th Infantry Regiment (commanded by Colonel Taylor) from the « Big Red One » set foot on Omaha's eastern portion (Easy and Fox sectors). The mission entrusted to these veterans was to neutralise the German defences, to open gateways from the beach inland (Saint-Laurent and Colleville) and to advance whilst weakening pockets of enemy resistance. As in Vierville, the strong tidal current had pushed the unit's landing craft eastwards. As a result, the landing operation was confused, units intermingling amidst the shellfire, landing barges alight, the whole scene under relentless machine gunfire.

Hence commenced an appalling nightmare for the assailants, a strange operation that had nothing in common with the one their chiefs had described: where were the bomb craters that were to offer shelter, where were the tanks that were to provide an armoured shield for the columns of infantrymen and that were to destroy the resistance nests, why were the enemy defences intact after preliminary bombings?

■ US troops on their way to Omaha in a landing barge

OMAHA BEACH

THE REASONS BEHIND THE CHAOS

The poor weather conditions on the morning of the 6th of June were, without a doubt, the reason for much of the assailants' disillusion.

The force 4 wind that was blowing in the English Channel on the dawn of the 6th of June, swelling the high waves to a height of 5 feet, was responsible for the wreck of most of the amphibious DD tanks that had been put to sea several miles off the coast, together with the Dukw trucks transporting the allied artillery. Similarly, the rough seas hindered the manoeuvres of special LCT craft in charge of overwhelming enemy defences by firing thousands of rockets immediately prior to the first influx of troops.

The skies were no more obliging and the heavy cloud that covered the Calvados beaches prevented any visual bombing. Consequently, flying at an altitude of 10,000 feet, the pilots of the 8th Air Force's 450 B24 aircraft had to carry out blind bombing guided only by the radar image of the narrow strip of coast, a highly arbitrary bombing technique, generally used on vast targets such as the Reich's harbour bastions. Furthermore, the pilots needed to bear in mind that whilst the 20,000 bombs targeting Omaha were being dropped, dozens of landing craft, spilling over with the troops that formed the first wave of attack, were less than 3,000 metres from the drop zone, in other words, barely thirty seconds at cruising speed. The greatest of care was therefore required to ensure that no more Americans than Germans accidentally fell victim to their attacks. In brief, an unsatisfactory bombing technique together with exaggerated caution resulted in not one single bomb hitting the German defences at Omaha!

Bombardments carried out by the US Navy warships anchored off the coast proved to be more effective. However, barely half an hour to bombard the 60 targets that Gerow had assigned to the Navy was quite insufficient. At Tarawa in 1943, the naval bom-

■ General Bradley, commander of the 1st US Army (on the left) with General Collins.

bing of Japanese defences had lasted three hours! The short timescale given to the US Navy demonstrates Bradley's strategy to exploit, both for the assault and the landing of reinforcements and equipment, as much daylight as possible; a total of 16 hours from dawn to dusk.

However the hostile elements do not fully explain the ordeal that the men from the V Corps (Gerow) went through on D-Day: human decisions or errors were to prove catastrophic. One might wonder how sailors could put themselves in such a vulnerable position among the strong Channel currents, or even how certain large LCT commanders could authorise dozens of amphibious tanks to be put to sea 3,000 metres from the shore in force 4 gales and heavy swell, whilst others, less reckless, did not hesitate to challenge the enemy guns by grounding on the shore before landing tanks and covering the infantrymen with their full firing potential.

More concerned about strategic success

■ Allied bombers

than tactical details, Gerow's chief, Bradley, commander of the 1st Army, had asked the 8th Air Force not to use highly powerful bombs on Omaha, convinced that such explosives would create huge craters, transforming the beach into a lunar landscape, in spite of the fact that they were the only weapons capable of damaging the concrete fortifications. Such excavations, similar to those still visible today at Pointe du Hoc, would hinder the progression of vehicles, causing congestion and paralysing the advancement inland. In brief, preliminary aerial bombardment should not jeopardise the assault, the main goal being to ensure the success of Overlord. Hence the decision to bombard Omaha with lightweight bombs, capable only of breaching barbed wire fencing, exploding mines or perhaps killing the defending German soldiers.

The final unpleasant surprise for the assailants was the discovery of a German division previously unmentioned in the Intelligence service's estimation of enemy numbers. Instead of the 716th Division's

■ Artillery from an American warship

600 aged or maimed soldiers, the Americans were in fact faced with 1,200 infantrymen from the 352nd Division, a unit that had been posted on the Calvados coast, between Arromanches and Vire, around three months prior to D-Day! Mobile, well-equipped and perfectly trained, the 352nd Division, which had fought on the Russian front, was to prove its great fighting merit on that morning of the 6th of June. Failure to detect the presence of the 352nd Division remains one of the greatest military errors by the allied secret services on the Western Front.

■ Channel coast surveillance

■ Allied warship off the Normandy coast on the morning of the 6th of June

■ Morning of the 6th of June, on Omaha Beach

REVERSING THE SITUATION

Since it appeared impossible to follow the plan which involved gaining access to the gullies to lead the way inland, another solution had to be found enabling troops to attack the fortifications from the rear. Two chiefs, General Norman Cota, second in command of the 29th Division and the most elderly soldier to land on Dog Green (Vierville) on the morning of the 6th of June, together with Colonel George Taylor, commander of the 1st Division's 16th Infantry Regiment landed at Colleville, were to break the deadlock via their initiative to scale the escarpment rather than to use the natural exits provided by the gullies. « If you stay on the beach, you're dead or about to die ».

Once they had heartened the spirits of their men, who were no longer fighting the enemy, but purely fighting to survive, teams of volunteers started to climb up the steep ridge. By mid morning, after an audacious ascent, a battalion from the 16th Infantry Regiment destroyed two particularly problematic resistance nests. On the opposite side of the shore, after having captured Vierville, General Cota started clearing the way for the largest beach exit.

However, the US Navy destroyers were to provide the decisive attack. Approaching the shoreline (at less than 1,000 metres), the destroyers used their guns to annihilate the enemy resistance nests, one after another. The arrival of mass reinforcements brought ashore by large LCTs was to definitively reverse the situation whilst, on the beach, German defence was weakening, with reserve troops sent to hunt out the paratroopers who had been drooped inland behind the 352nd Division, and with lacking armoured tanks around Caen. Taking advantage of the front, sappers on

■ The assault on Omaha

■ Landing craft tank
off Omaha beach

the beach created corridors amidst the minefields, filled the antitank ditches and organised exits, « It was a miracle … ».

By the time night had fallen, the Germans had lost the battle on the beach and the Americans were, as yet, unaware that they had won. General Gerow, Commander of the V Corps, then landed and set up his command post on the summit of the ridge dominating the vast beach where over 1,500 soldiers lay dead, representing half of total D-Day losses. Measuring 8 kilometres long and only 2 kilometres deep (rather than 25 by 10), the Omaha bridgehead was still relatively vulnerable and totally isolated between Utah and Gold. Two days later, Omaha joined the British bridgehead and, on the 12th of June, the neighbouring Utah beach. The following day, the 1st Division that had suffered such great losses on Omaha captured Caumont l'Eventé, a bocage village located over 30 kilometres from the coast. Such a spectacular advance towards Saint-Lô was, for the V Corps, a remarkable revival.

■ Reinforcements arrive on Omaha

THE ATTACK ON POINTE DU HOC

LA POINTE DU HOC

1 - Firing command post
2 - Platform
3 - Casemate
4 - Shelter or ammunition store
5 - Anti-air defence construction

■ Map of the Pointe du Hoc artillery battery

Together with the raids launched by British paratroopers on the night of the 5th to the 6th of June on the Merville battery and Bénouville bridge (Pegasus Bridge), the American assault on Pointe du Hoc was one of D-Day's most extraordinary achievements. The capture of the coastal artillery battery at Pointe du Hoc, by an American Rangers commando, remains one of the most audacious operations ever undertaken in military history.

POINTE DU HOC ARTILLERY BATTERY

Built at the summit of a rocky cliff, at half a dozen kilometres from Vierville, the famous battery was capable of scouring the areas surrounding both Omaha and Utah. Similarly to many other German artillery positions (Mont Canisy, Houlgate,

■ French-made 15.5cm gun from the Hoc artillery battery

■ Sentry on the Normandy coast

24

■ Bessin cliffs: Pointe du Hoc and its Channel headland

Ouistreham and Maisy), the Hoc battery was equipped with six large guns made in France. As on other sites along the Normandy coastline, these pieces of artillery, of a 15.5cm calibre and a maximum range of 20,000 metres, had originally been placed, uncovered, on circular concrete platforms of a diameter of over 16 metres. In the autumn of 1943, following several aerial bombardments, the German command decided to shelter the guns in huge bunkers. In the spring of 1944, only two casemates were complete (bunkers endowed with a large window or gap known as a gun port to enable firing), however the pieces of artillery had not yet been installed inside. Close to the platforms and firing blocks, scattered shelters provided quarters for the 150 men comprising the garrison together with a few ammunition stores. The fortifications were linked to each other by means of underground corridors or trenches which also provided access to the firing command post. This last half-entrenched bunker is located on the edge of the cliff overlooking the sea. On the ground floor were the map room and the observation post with binoculars fitted to a tripod and, on the first floor (in fact situated at ground level), the open-air telemetry post. Defended by several machine gun nests, surrounded by minefields and barbed wire fencing, totally cut off from the outside world, Hoc was one of the Atlantic Wall's solid Stützpunkt (strong points). This small Festung (fortress) appeared to be impregnable.

■■■ FIRMER AND MORE STRUCTURED RESISTANCE

■ In the foreground to the left, the Battleship Texas which fired its 35cm guns and 250 huge shells on Pointe du Hoc on the morning of the 6th of June from 5.50 to 6.30am. The Texas was hit by German artillery during the Cherbourg bombings on the 25th of June 1944

THE ATTACK ON THE FESTUNG

Due to its excellent position and the firing range of its guns, ensuring the control of coastal navigation in the western portion of the Seine Bay, Point du Hoc had to be eliminated. Just as the Merville battery in the British sector was capable of ruining the assault on Sword Beach, the Hoc guns were capable of transforming the American landings into a nightmare.

■ Antitank ditch

The Rangers

The operation consisted in landing a small troop at the foot of the cliff at either side of the point, scaling the sheer precipice, destroying the guns and advancing inland to establish a barrage on the coastal Grandcamp - Vierville road, hence preventing any German reinforcements to be brought to Omaha Beach. This perilous mission was entrusted to Colonel Rudder and 225 elite soldiers from the 2nd Rangers Battalion. Barely had Rudder learned of his mission, he started training his men on the Isle of Wight cliffs. It was during such training exercises that the spe-

■ American Rangers at Pointe du Hoc

cial climbing equipment was determined (rope ladders, grappling launchers...)

A rough crossing

Towards 4.30am, the LCA fleet transporting the Rangers set off for its target approximately ten nautical miles away. The choppy seas, a strong coastal current and, apparently, some difficulty in distinguishing Pointe du Hoc from Pointe de La Percée, caused the convoy to drift east-wards towards Omaha. Aerial and naval bombardments by the 9th US Air Force Marauders and the US Navy had ceased immediately before 6.30am, the hour initially planned for the Rangers' assault. However, the navigation error taking time to correct, Rudder delayed the assault by 40 minutes. This delay apparently left sufficient time for the defenders to gather their wits and, by 7.10am, the German artillerymen were ready and waiting to welcome Rudder's fleet which was making its approach parallel to the shoreline. Due to the loss of several landing craft during the long crossing, the attack, initially planned from both sides of the point, was made only from the eastern flank.

■ Pointe du Hoc casemate, 6th June 1944

Attack!

Despite showers of grenades and gunfire, the Rangers fired rocket-propelled grappling hooks, to which rope ladders were attached, towards the crest of the cliff. Five minutes after landing, the first allied soldier set foot on the plateau summit and twenty minutes later, the 150 surviving Rangers reached their target. After tremendous effort and great human sacrifice, the assailants were staggered to discover that the artillery position was totally devoid of guns! Similarly to Riva, in the Orne estuary, artillery had been moved and hidden in a small pathway a kilometre further south. The Germans had installed huge beams in the gun emplacements and had covered them with swathes of camouflage netting. As soon as the defenders, who had taken refuge in the labyrinth of underground corridors, were under control, the Rangers advanced inland, found the guns, destroyed them, then established defence positions in case of a counter attack.

■ Allied bomber formation above Pointe du Hoc on Tuesday 25th of April, at approximately 6pm. This bombing operation was to destroy two gun emplacements and damage three of the six guns. Following these bombardments, the guns were removed from their platforms and hidden in a small pathway further inland.

THE ARTIFICIAL US HARBOUR ON OMAHA BEACH

As early as the day after D-Day, the English Channel set the scene for the greatest ever towing operation in history with the creation of two artificial harbours, code-named Mulberries. One of them, located in Arromanches, was designed to provide fresh supplies for the British Army, the other, located on Omaha beach, for the American Army. At Omaha, in order to break the English Channel's typically heavy swell, allied engineers had designed an artificial bombardon, to be built at high seas, approximately 2 nautical miles from the coast facing Vierville-Colleville and comprising two elements: blockships and Phoenix caissons. The blockships, designed to be sunk on the seabed, were submerged one after another as from the 7th of June, forming a line parallel to the shore. Providing a primary breakwater, they offered a sheltered zone for cargoes during the days following the assault. Baptised Gooseberry, this nascent barrier was extended and reinforced with huge concrete cubes, referred to as Phoenix caissons (similar caissons can be seen to this day at Arromanches).

As in any maritime port, the Mulberry, located in the heart of a vast stretch of water behind the bombardon, housed mooring quays for unloading merchant ships. The platforms comprising the quays had the particularity of being attached to large vertical piles along which they oscillated in time with the ebb and flow of the tide, hence enabling unloading operations to be continued without interruption.

By the 10th of June, all of the blockships had been submerged on the seabed. A week later, 32 of the planned 51 caissons were in place, together with an open pile quay upon which, on the same day, an LST unloaded 11,000 men and 2,000 vehicles. On the 19th of June, a violent storm was to rise in the English Channel and, after 3 days of blustering winds, Omaha artificial harbour had been reduced to a pile of torn and tangled iron. At the end of the month, following the capture of the port of Cherbourg, General Eisenhower decided not to have Omaha harbour rebuilt.

■ Deprived of an artificial harbour, the Americans were to unload their supplies directly onto Utah and Omaha beaches.

■ View of Omaha artificial harbour on the 18th of June 1944. The open pile quay and the floating roadway can be seen in the foreground.

THE AMERICAN CEMETERY IN COLLEVILLE-SUR-MER A PLACE OF GLORY, A PLACE OF MEMORY

■ The American Military Cemetery overlooking Omaha Beach and the English Channel

A place of glory for the heroes who fell on the battlefield in Normandy throughout the summer of 1944, a place of memory for today's generations who owe their freedom to those who are laid to rest there; such is the message conveyed by the American cemetery in Colleville-sur-Mer. The Normandy American Cemetery, situated on the summit of the plateau dominating Omaha Beach, was inaugurated in June 1956 by President Coty and General Marshall. France has indefinitely donated this 70 hectare parcel of territory to the United States as a symbol of its gratitude.

Today, the necropolis is the eternal home to some 10,000 American soldiers, killed during landing operations and throughout the weeks that followed. Within this vast rectangle, parallel to the shoreline, the graves of the heroes who fell in the name of freedom are divided into ten squares. Lined up like an army standing to attention, the white marble crosses on their immense green blanket leave an abiding impact on any visitor. How moving it is to find several American families with two sons, buried side by side, or father and son together, or even the graves of women, former US Army nurses and auxiliaries.

Besides the great squares of military graves, the cemetery also holds a chapel situated at the intersection of the main aisles, a memorial with colonnades and a

■ Aerial view of the American Cemetery stretching across 70 hectares In the background, the memorial and colonnade and, in the foreground, the pond and masts.

bronze statue symbolising the spirit of American youth and, finally, a visitor reception building. To the right of the large ornamental lake and the high masts that tower above the area reserved for ceremonies and patriotic events, an orienteering table has been installed at the summit of the escarpment overlooking the vast shore. And finally, in the rose garden behind the memorial colonnades, stands a wall bearing the names of over 1,550 lost soldiers from the 1st US Army (Bradley).

■ White marble cross on the green velvet lawn.

THE AMERICAN CEMETERY IN COLLEVILLE-SUR-MER A PLACE OF GLORY, A PLACE OF MEMORY

Visitors to this vast and imposing memorial park, with its meticulously pruned and nurtured gardens, ensuring year-long verdure, are left with an impression of greatness and tranquillity propitious to meditation. Although, with around 1 million visitors each year, one is rarely alone, the American Cemetery at Omaha Beach is one of those places where one's soul flies free.

Within this vast cemetery, a new building was opened in June 2007. Of simple, geometrical architecture, the construction, which gives the impression that it is directly linked to the Channel foreshore, is both an exhibition and a historical centre recounting the Battle of Normandy.

A second American cemetery (12 hectares) can be found in the Norman town of Saint-James. The cemetery is the last resting place of the GIs lost during the battle to free Saint-Lô in the course of operation « Cobra » (penetration of the German front to the west of Saint-Lô), during the German counter attack on Mortain and the violent combat in the Falaise pocket.

■ In the background: the wall in the garden of lost soldiers
■ Below: the « Visitor Center ».